The Traffic Formula

The Secret to Finding Raving Buyers

for Your E-Commerce Business

Without Spending Any Money on Ads!

DEIRDRE TSHIEN

ISBN: 9798734247143

Imprint: Independently published

TABLE OF CONTENTS

INTRODUCTION

I still remember the moment my husband and I decided to go "all-in." I was sitting on the couch watching TV and could hear Ash in the kitchen singing off-beat as he checked up on his latest dessert creation.

The sweet aroma of chocolate drifted into the living room. It made my shoulders relax and my mouth salivate, even though we had just finished eating dinner.

Ash had rediscovered his love of cooking and used it as a way to escape from his unhappiness at school. He was studying medicine and the workload was all-consuming. Our dinners also allowed me to temporarily forget about my disillusioned dreams of climbing the corporate ladder. Coming from an Asian family with strict expectations, I was following the "go to school, get spotless grades, get a good job" model, *and it was draining my soul.*

Those moments felt especially precious to both Ash and me because they were like a "time-out" from a perpetual cycle of work that was void of meaning and purpose.

Have you ever felt like that?

We were both unhappy in what we were doing, and had been talking on and off about potentially starting a business. But what could we do? How would we get started? When?

We had very little money, no ideas, no connections or business skills, and other than our desire to escape our current situation: we had no clue what to do.

But, back to chocolate. Ash brought his new creation into the living room. He had been working like a mad scientist, perfecting my all-time favorite dessert. It was something we used to travel half an hour for, served by an Italian restaurant in Sydney. He entered the room, and my jaw dropped as he presented it. It was a chocolate molten lava cake; a divine expression of otherworldly deliciousness that, when eaten, could ascend you to a higher plane of enlightenment. And it did!

It was over that particular dessert - which we ultimately named The Choc Pot - we made the decision to embark on our entrepreneurial journey. In that delicious moment of chocolatey heaven, we committed to open our own dessert bar, and take Sydney by storm!

You may wonder why I'm telling you this story. Isn't this book meant to be about growing an e-commerce business and increasing your traffic? Yes, it is. It's also about building a long-term brand that impacts people's lives. It's for people who aren't in business just for the money, or because they hate their job and don't want to answer to a boss.

I'm assuming you have a burning passion towards your craft, products, or services that you offer. Which means you've already passed the first step to building a thriving brand!

Passion for your products is the first characteristic you must have in order to create an amazing business. Your products are a reflection of that passion. Since my mission is helping you transfer your love of those products into the minds and hearts of your customers, I'd like to clarify who this book is for.

If you're an absolute beginner, you will get key insights that will help you set up a strong foundation for your e-commerce brand. If your business is still a side-hustle and you want to transition into a full-time entrepreneur, you'll get strategies for increasing your traffic and sales to finally make the switch to "all in." If you're running your business full-time, and have hit a ceiling that feels impossible to break through, you'll gain ways to maximize your current resources to increase growth. If you want to scale well beyond your current business, you'll get a framework for attracting more visitors to your online storefront and sell more of your products.

This three-book series will show you how to optimize and scale your e-commerce business to maximize your profitability, without compromising your sanity!

You may wonder how this book series fits together. So, firstly, this book will teach you the fundamentals of creating an irresistible offer and leveraging a unique process we call *The Traffic Pyramid*. You'll use it to find your cold ideal audience, make them curious about you and then start converting them.

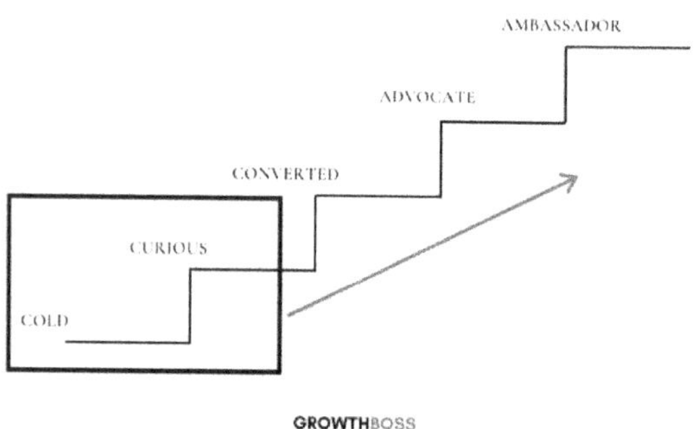

In the second book, we're going to be talking tribe building and conversions. We're going to build upon the Traffic Pyramid and use emails and the Live Conversion Method™ to supercharge conversions en masse. We will also be delving into how to create your advocates and ambassadors; leveraging fans to become your raving salesforce!

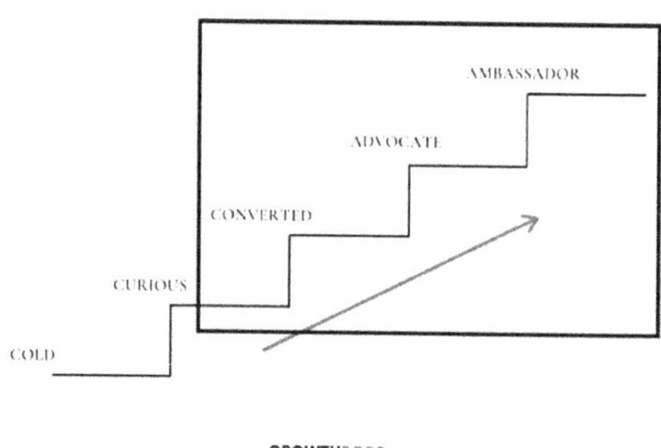

In book 3, we're now on all the channels your ideal audience is hanging out at, and we're going to dominate the conversation on all these platforms effectively, on autopilot! We're going to do that through an effective process we call Content Storytelling, so that you are talking to the hearts and minds of your audience, having them know, like and trust you so they never feel the need to go to anyone else.

Since the technology and media landscape change so frequently, I'm making these concepts as evergreen as possible. I will be talking predominantly about strategy, frameworks, and models that you can use regardless of changes to social media. If you become obsessed with the strategy and not the platform, you can make intelligent choices going forward.

IDENTIFY YOUR AUDIENCE

The most essential factor in our business's success is how we interact with our customers. We attract them, compel them to buy our products, keep them satisfied for as long as possible, and inspire them to share information about our brand and products with friends and family. Without them, our business cannot survive. *Actually, without them, we do not have a business!*

You could have the best products in the world, with all your systems and technology set up to deliver them efficiently. However, without reaching the right people and compelling them to buy from you, your hard work will not pay off. You must master the skill of profitably acquiring and keeping customers for life. And then having them rave about you! Let me tell you about how I learned this…

A couple of years into having launched our first business, The Choc Pot, I was still working a corporate job. It was an investment bank in Sydney. Around that time, I had joined a new team. I only knew one person in that team. To bring us all together, our manager arranged a meet-and-greet event, so we could get to know each other.

It was a sunny, warm day in Sydney and I was standing on the balcony with two other members of my new team. James was the one person I already knew because we were acquaintances who had hung out in similar circles during University. Nic, I didn't know at all, but I remember how animated he was. He had us in tears, laughing.

As we were chatting, Nic suddenly turned to us and said, "Oh, I went to this amazing place last night with some friends. It was started by this couple. The guy was studying medicine and wasn't enjoying it, but he loved baking and was perfecting this dessert, called a choc pot, for his girlfriend. And from that they started this business. Isn't that so cool?!"

I was incredibly embarrassed because I hate that type of attention (even though at the time he didn't know I was the girlfriend in the story)! You might not be able to pick it up, but I'm a massive introvert.

Of course, James wasn't going to let it go. He knew me, our story, and turned to Nic saying, "Yeah Nic, don't you know it's her?" He was pointing at me! I'm pretty sure I was smiling awkwardly, shifting from foot to foot, avoiding eye contact, and I don't blame Nic for being totally confused.

Then, Nic tried being helpful by clarifying: "I'm talking about this couple. He was studying medicine and gave it up so that they could start a dessert bar. It's called The Choc Pot. You guys have to go try it!" James pointed at me again, and emphasized, "Yeah dude! It's her!"

At the time, it made me incredibly embarrassed, but I just have to laugh about it now. I just needed to learn to be ok with becoming the face of the business, which I really struggled with back then. And I know for some of you who went into e-commerce, you might similarly struggle with becoming the face of your business, too. But trust me: apply what you'll be learning in this series, and not only will you become incredibly comfortable building this human connection, you will come to love it!

Looking back, what I particularly love about this story with Nic is that, without even realizing it at the time, I had created a "buyer ladder" and had someone literally standing in front of me moving up it, and raving about us, selling us to other people!

I want to walk you through the Buyer Ladder so that you have the basis from which our whole strategy will follow.

THE BUYER LADDER

Before we get started, let's address a few myths regarding marketing. There's a common misconception that certain people are born gifted at sales and marketing. That, in order to be successful in business, you need to be born with it. This is a flawed theory. Nobody is born a natural salesperson, entrepreneur, or marketer. These are skillsets. They're something you develop.

Another myth is that you need to *push,* hard sell, or do something out of alignment with your ethics. Again, this is false! I'm going to share with you a concept that helps build a relationship with your audience so they know, like, and trust you *before* you ever ask them to buy something. This concept is called *The Buyer Ladder.*

The *Buyer Ladder* is a series of 'stairs' your audience progresses through on their journey as a customer. Our objective is moving them to the next stair on the ladder. It's all about moving them from "Cold" to "Curious," to "Converted," to "Advocates," and finally becoming your "Ambassadors." Let me show you what I mean (I hinted to it earlier).

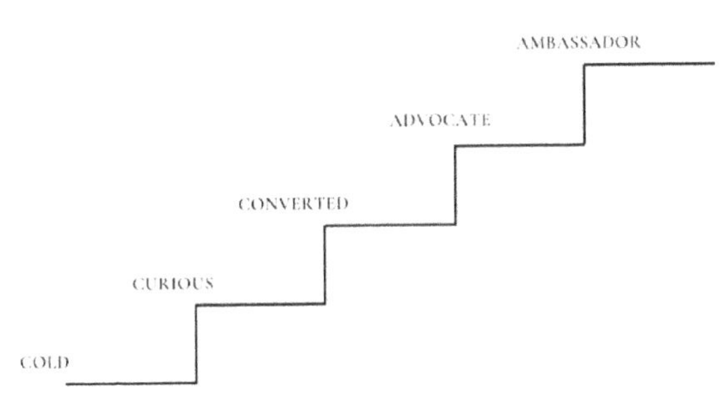

Let's review each stage.

Cold Audience. This is when a particular person has never heard about you. They are strangers; unaware of you, your brand, products and services. Another term you might hear for your audience at this stage is that they are at the "top of your funnel." That is, they haven't entered your world yet. Our purpose here is to bring them into your sphere of influence.

Curious Audience. This is when someone has entered your sphere of influence to become aware of your brand and what you do. You may know this as "lead-generation." It's like meeting someone for the first time. They were a stranger and now you've piqued their interest. There isn't necessarily a high level of trust. But there's enough familiarity to at least share their email, look at your products, and assess the value. Perhaps they came across your social media page and clicked over your site, saw an ad, joined your group, or your email list. They now know you, but they have not yet bought anything. They are just curious about you and what you do.

Converted Audience. At this stage, you have developed enough trust and rapport with your audience for them to pull the trigger and buy something from you. You *converted* your audience from a lead into a sale. In e-commerce, there are so many amazing ways to do this. This is the topic we're going to explore in more detail within the second book.

Advocates. These are your raving fans! They love you. They feel connected to you and your brand. They also feel a sense of loyalty. They are repeat customers who will tell anyone that will listen how good you and your products are. Spoiler alert: we want a lot of these!

Ambassadors. These are the raving fans who would love to share about you, but just need a little bit more of a nudge – an incentive – so you can create referrals and social proof at scale. Your ambassadors will complete certain tasks on your behalf and will be incentivized for creating incredibly valuable social currency.

So, how do we put a Buyer Ladder into effect? How do we apply this framework into something that helps us get traffic? The first answer is: your audience needs to connect with you in order to go from Cold to Ambassadors. That boils down to your customer's *avatar*, or *persona*.

KNOW YOUR AVATAR

One of the common mistakes people make while creating (or improving) their brand is to immediately start content creation, without doing any groundwork upfront. They start posting on social media and hope something works. Yet, hope is not a strategy. We want to be able to take as much control of the selling process as possible. That's why we teach *context* over *content.* In this section, we're going to define your target customer. Since everything revolves around them, that's the *context* we'll base all the messaging and offers on (*content*). Let's start with the basics.

WHO AND WHERE ARE THEY?

The first thumbnail sketch you want to clarify is your ideal customer's demographics. These are characteristics you can easily define like their age, gender, income, family size, location, ethnicity, education level, etc. Take a moment and think about them.

Next, what are their psychographics? These are your customer's values, interests, hobbies, political affiliations, lifestyle perceptions, religious or spiritual views, attitude and personality. Also, what gets them emotional? Think about what makes your customers feel strongly. Those emotions could be positive or negative. The key distinction about emotions is that they're *charged.* For instance, what do they *worry* about most? What do they secretly *fear* or absolutely *resent*? What causes them a tremendous sense of emotional pain, frustration, shame, guilt, or overwhelming pride, confidence and accomplishment? When no one is watching, what do they envision, want, and desire most? How would your ideal customer answer the following phrase:

"If I could finally ___ then I would be able to ____"?

We want to change the rules of the game in a way that turns commodities into must-haves. If you essentially sell the same product as someone else, by getting far into the customer's mind, we're able to position our products in a way they find impossible to ignore.

Go deep with this, give your person a name and a personality. Find a photo of this person. Make them real. And then going forward, know that you must run every business decision past this person (or at least through their lens).

I dug around and found the avatars for my first couple of businesses. Every marketing message, our tone of voice, our brand personality came about because we knew deeply who this person was and what they wanted.

THE CHOC POT CUSTOMER

Meet **Ally** – she's 24 years old and is super social, loves life and having fun. She leads a balanced lifestyle, staying healthy and fit in order to enjoy indulging herself.

She loves to travel and doing outdoor activities, aspiring to chase waterfalls through hiking. She is also an avid yogi.

She spends a most of her time with her friends, boyfriend or family, leading a very social and full life. She is lively, fun, energetic and optimistic. She always looks at the positive side of things.

She likes to post on Instagram (because if it's not on Insta, it didn't happen right?) about her travel escapades, weekends away, #squadgoals and food.

THE STAX ON CUSTOMER

Meet **Steve** – he's 23 years old and is super social, loves going to the gym. He can't cook or is lazy about cooking, but he's discerning about the food he eats.

He is a closet nerd (likes superhero movies and Star Wars). He's into rap and hip hop (e.g. Kendrick Lamar, Wutan Clan, Kanye West, Drake and Jay Z), but also isn't afraid to admit he likes some pop (e.g. Justin Timberlake, Ed Sheeren, Maroon 5).

He watches a lot of sports like NBA, NFL, soccer and likes to be "fly" with his new sneakers and snapbacks.

He likes to post on Instagram and Snapchat about his gym gains, travel and food.

He's also a little addicted to watching cat videos…

These are thinking exercises for you to continue using from this point forward. They're a habit you do constantly as a way of creating new breakthroughs in your business. These are not a one-time event where you sit down to think of them, and you're done. They're an ongoing process that expands throughout your time as an e-commerce entrepreneur. In fact, as you start ascending the Traffic Pyramid, you will experience just how *alive* this process is! Let's take this even further.

WHAT'S THEIR BEFORE AND AFTER?

Our aspirations, desires, and wants are (almost) always based in the future. We're *here* now. We're going *there.* When we get *there,* our desires are fulfilled. We feel comfort, security, alleviation of pain, and happier. It's this connection to a future outcome that creates an internal attraction for buying products.

Think about it for a minute. Why did you buy this book? There are specific reasons you could report. At a superficial level, "I want more traffic to my site," may be one. Yet, if we dig a little deeper, there's more to it than just traffic. Getting more traffic is connected to earning money, and less frustration. It's also connected to a sense of achievement, and *certainty* that you're doing the right thing, and not the wrong thing. When it comes to getting more traffic, you have your own desire that is unique to you. It's the story you tell yourself (subconsciously) about why getting this book was a good choice. That subconscious process is what we call *mapping out the before and after.*

Imagine being able to step into your potential customer's perspective for a month, or so. You would see exactly what they do in their daily life and experience that for yourself. Yet, you would have the advantage of not being emotionally attached. The result of this "experience in empathy" would be understanding and feeling more compassion toward them. You would have the ability to observe their thoughts, know exactly which images appeal to their senses. You'd also know which ones they find repelling, too.

Question: what would that level of understanding, empathy, and compassion enable you to do? Reflect on it for just a moment.

Now, imagine being able to come back into your own perspective. You are *you* again; the talented ecommerce owner you are ☺. However, when you get back, you are a better, more talented ecommerce owner because you now also have the wisdom you gained by empathizing.

This distinction has the power to impact *everything* you do in your business: from the quality of the products, to enhancing the delivery time, to customer support, follow-up, content creation, advertising, and more. It would change which words you use, and the way you use them. It would affect the imagery on your site and your social media, too. Literally, every aspect of your brand would change. That experience would shift all points of contact you share with your customers as they progress on their buyer ladder journey.

Mapping the before and after gives you the ability to help your potential customers envision the life-changing after-effects of your products and services. Not only will they embrace those positive qualities of that future result, they'll also feel a tremendous sense of internal tension between that desire and the mediocrity of life before. That's when your products and offers sell like crazy. That's when your potential customer lands on your site, not just thinking about the features or price, but fantasizing and craving what their life is going to look, feel, and sound like when they experience the after effects.

It could be a cooling face wash after a hot summer day and feeling refreshed, relaxed, and ready for a social gathering. It could be the sense of connectedness, acceptance, and love they get from bringing the baked goodies to their friend after a rough patch in their relationship. Make them go starry eyed and show them by painting a picture in their minds!

In Growth Boss's 3-day Cold to Converted Challenge one of the first exercises I walk our participants through is helping them determine whether your product is a "painkiller" or a "vitamin." I ask our participants: "Is your product positioned to help your customer move away from pain, or move toward pleasure?"

At the core of human motivation, we have two basic patterns. The first is that we move away from pain. The second is that we move toward pleasure. If you want people to buy your products, you'll need to determine what the primary driver is for your customer and talk to that effectively in your marketing.

Think about this with something basic: taxes. If you don't file your taxes by x date, you're going to suffer a penalty. If you don't know how to file your taxes properly, you're going to spend more money than you need to. You'll also waste a ton of time. These three facts are what drive accounting firms' sales, QuickBooks, and other accounting software. Those services and products help you stay organized and therefore: out of trouble (painkiller).

People don't buy a skincare, nutrition, or workout product because they love *possessing* them. That psychological need for acceptance is running in the background at all times. We want to look good. Why? Because we want to be accepted by our peers. Why? Because we're afraid of not being loved and accepted. We're afraid of being left out or worse: *left behind*. A core desire for humans is validation. Hence people go through extraordinary measures to fit in and be "good enough" to avoid the pain of exclusion, which is oftentimes attached to our materiality.

Painkillers relieve pain. Vitamin products add something to our lives. What type of product do you have? Are you helping someone move away from a problem they have in their lives, or are you helping them move towards an aspiration, a goal? Make a bullet point list of the symptoms and different ways they manifest. How does it affect your customers relationships, money, satisfaction, self-esteem, or time? What are they thinking, feeling, saying or doing right now, before they've received your product, when they've received your product, while they're using it and finally when they get the result that they are after?

In fashion and accessories, not having the right outfit could inhibit Mary's ability to speak to her boss confidently. It might make her feel self-conscious among her colleagues. What's life currently like now? And then speak into the positive future. Continuing Mary's example: it's that moment when Mary walks into the room, and someone notices her. She's walking through the doorway into the office, or the online meeting, and her coworker gives her a compliment. It's the moment when she can stride (not walk) into a meeting with her boss, it's the moment at which she notices that she's smiling at herself more frequently in the bathroom mirror (vitamin).

There is a Growth Boss in my Academy, Christine, who sells dog bows and bandanas. She used to struggle with thinking through the result she's trying to get her customer. "I just sell dog bows", she used to say. But she doesn't just sell dog bows. She sells the fact that dogs deserve to feel confident too.

We're not consciously making these assessments. We're never like, "Oh, I want this product because I really want some external validation, or because I want to avoid being mocked and laughed at." All those feelings happen beneath the surface of our consciousness. We never know consciously what the underlying root-cause is… we only ever think or feel the symptoms.

Think like a doctor. As a doctor, when someone walks into your office, they say, "I have a headache. I'm dizzy and tired. I can't sleep." You hear what they're saying, and you understand those are symptoms. Those symptoms are top of mind. Those symptoms they're feeling - before they've tried your painkiller or vitamin product - are how you will talk about your customer's Before point.

WHAT SYMPTOMS ARE THEY FEELING?

When you empathize and speak to someone about their symptoms – almost better than they can in their own words – you build immediate trust and rapport, which is why it's such an effective marketing tool. However, how do you go from empathizing with their symptoms to getting them to buy your product? The answer is to move them through the stages of the buying decision-making process: being symptom-aware, to problem-aware, to solution-aware.

I asked you to think like a doctor in the previous section. When someone comes into your office and says "I have a headache. I'm dizzy and tired. I can't sleep", they are relaying their symptoms. Here, they are symptom-aware. They are aware of the things that they are thinking, feeling and doing at their Before point.

They are not yet problem-aware, until you, as the doctor, diagnose them. Perhaps the cause of their symptoms – the "problem" - is that they have a brain tumor (not to be extreme or anything…) This is the reason they are feeling those symptoms. Once you have diagnosed them, they become problem-aware. They know now what is causing the pain they have been feeling.

Once they know what their problem is, they're going to want to fix it! And this is when they become solution-aware. They will want the painkiller or the vitamin you're offering because it is going to help them relieve the symptoms they've been feeling, and remove the cause of their problem. This is how we go from talking to someone's symptoms, building that trust and rapport with them, to having them buy our product, and get them to their After point.

For anyone with a vitamin product, where you are moving someone towards pleasure, you might be reading this getting stuck on the word "problem". Because you might think you don't help solve a problem. And this is when I would encourage you to go back to the symptoms. At the point in time when they realize they need to buy your product, what are they thinking, saying, feeling and doing? If you sell indoor plants, is it that they are feeling the emptiness and lack of life inside a room or an apartment? If you sell scrunchies and hair bows, is it because they wanted to feel a connection with their daughter through doing her hair with something pretty?

One of my Growth Bosses, Anu, is a curator of beautiful South-East Asian art. Her customers currently feel uninspired by their surroundings and want to create an environment that is uplifting, calming and striking all at the same time.

We are all feeling something when we make a purchase. There is always a reason behind it. You might just need to dig a little deeper to find yours.

Because once you can empathize with the symptoms your ideal customers are feeling, then moving them to buy through your marketing messages becomes infinitely simpler.

To move them to buy, we need to start tapping into their emotions. And to do this, we need to "paint the picture."

HOW DO YOU PAINT THE PICTURE?

A few years before we made the move to New York City, Ash and I came to visit for a holiday in the spring. It was the second time we had been to NYC and it was a different experience because we had gotten the "touristy stuff" out of our system already.

This time, we found a small place in Chelsea to stay. We experienced the city as a local. We found an amazing bagel breakfast spot (the café on 22nd Ash couldn't stay away from). We had our afternoon walk routes on the Highline and the Greenway. We experienced all sorts of New York magic.

We were on one of our walks back from the Greenway, on a non-descript street. It was my favorite time in the twilight hours of that spring evening. The sun was close to setting and the sky was turning into a beautiful pinkish-orange color. People started turning on their lights in their houses, families were starting to settle down for the night together, and there was an optimism, love, and beauty in the air. Then, Ash turned to me and asked me something that I believe changed the trajectory of our lives. He said "could you imagine living here and these were our evenings?"

With that one question, I knew this was where I was meant to be at some point. He managed to take everything we were hearing, seeing and feeling, and boil it down to one question that vividly painted the picture for me. And from that, I was swept away. The vision was in my mind and I couldn't let it go. And a few short years later, we made the move.

I've always been fascinated with what makes people buy. This is the stuff I geek out about. And after having gone through that experience myself, I know how powerful it is to paint the picture for someone.

Your customers must envision themselves getting a result from your solutions (literally, a subconscious vision). So, as much as you can, paint a picture for them. Use your stories, language and imagery that shakes them out of their "conserve energy, stay in comfort mode," and compels them to get the benefits you're offering from your products.

What does the "promised land" look like for them? What transformation can you help them achieve by relieving their symptoms and helping them solve their problem (or reach their aspiration) with your product.

If you can do this, you are making it so much easier for them to make the mental leap to just buy because you are starting to tap into their *emotions*, the primary driver for all our decision-making. Your potential customers need to know that they don't have to be someone else, be somewhere else, to achieve what they want to. They don't have to fundamentally change who they are in order to get to that "After" point you are promising them. You're already starting to lower the automatic barriers they put up to resist buying.

A great example of this is saranoni.com. They sell blankets. But blankets are a means to an end. That end isn't "keep your body warm." It's the future vision of a cuddle party with your son or daughter. It's a Sunday, connecting with your family. The people at Saranoni.com are absolutely brilliant at painting pictures like that, and selling their vitamin product.

If you want to paint a picture for your audience, how would you go about it?

Here's an exercise that will help...

1. Make a bullet-pointed list about the demographics and psychographics of your ideal customer. What is their age, gender, location, income, etc. What do they identify with in terms of affiliations, their political views, religious views, etc.?

2. In paragraph form, write what a day FEELS like in their life. The purpose of this is building as much empathy as possible with this person.

3. Give a single name to your most ideal customer. "Allow me to introduce you to Annie… Patrick… Susan… (Whomever)." Give your ideal customer a name that brings them to life for you and your team.

4. On a single sheet of paper, write "moving toward" and "Moving away from."

5. Place a line between the two.

6. List as many symptoms as you can in the "moving away from" column.

7. Start vividly describing what their "promised land" or transformation will be with your product in the "moving toward" column. Paint the picture for them.

KEY TAKEAWAYS:

- The Buyer Ladder is a series of steps that defines your customer's engagement with you (from "Cold" to "Curious," "Converted," to "Advocates," and finally becoming your "Ambassadors").
- The more you know about your target audience, the clearer you'll be about which marketing media and strategies you should invest your time in.
- Map out your target audience by building a customer avatar: know their demographics and psychographics, as well as the symptoms they're experiencing as the result of not buying your product.
- Any time you're planning a marketing campaign, keep your avatar at the forefront of your imagination. Write out their "before and after", know deeply the symptoms they are feeling and emotionally connect that to your products and services by "painting the picture."

MAGNETIZE YOUR AUDIENCE

Sometimes I love playing the "remember when…" game. It always takes me back to that different time in my life in high school, when things felt simpler.

I have so many memories I cherish; the piggy back races, the mini-soccer tournaments, the pranks, the laughter. I remember the sun on my face as we were lazing on the hill at lunch-time.

A moment I cherish (even though it was excruciating at the time), was when my now-husband and I "got together." Just thinking back to that moment makes me smile and cringe from the "high-schoolness" of it all!

I met my husband in high school, and yes, we are high school sweethearts. We liked each other for a while (since 7th grade) and by the time we were nearing the 9th grade, my friends were fed up with us. They devised a plan to get us alone on the train we used to catch together after school, and coerced me into finally just asking him if he liked me. It was excruciating!

And Ash's reply? "Yeah… why not".

Wow. Please knock me over with the romance of it all!

But it got the job done and we've been together ever since. And now, you might be wondering why I'm telling you this.

Just the other night, Ash and I were playing the "remember when…" game. I was asking him about how he knew he liked me back in 7th grade and when it had happened. And he was telling me about the great legs I had. Typical male.

Then, he started telling me about this dream that he had one night where he was walking down some rocks towards a beach, being drawn towards a girl. And when she turned around, it was me. And that was when he *really* noticed me in high school and started liking me. Because I had infiltrated his subconscious. And the reason why I wanted to tell you this is because this is how marketing essentially works.

Every relationship, no matter if it is a romantic one, a platonic one, one between a brand and its customer, a service-provider and their client… always starts with something that magnetizes them together; something that "hooks" them in.

For our relationship, it seemed to be my legs. I knew I was drawn to him because of his ease of playing sports. All completely superficial. But once you're drawn in, even without knowing it, the subconscious takes over. And it is then our job to make something happen! So, I wanted to start with helping you work out your business's equivalent of my legs.

In this section, we're going to explore ways to move your audience from Cold to Curious in your buyer ladder. We'll create a lead magnet that is going to draw your customer in so that you start to infiltrate their subconscious. We'll then find all the ways you can create and find this traffic of your audience so you can hook them in with your lead magnet - with the aim of continuing to stay in front of them so that the only thing they can say to you is… "yeah… why not."

CREATE YOUR LEAD MAGNET

I understand first-hand how seductive it can be to speak about your product, over and over and over again. I can bet that almost every post you might be doing right now is some kind of photo about your product, asking people to buy. And yet… you might be wondering why no one is buying.

This comes back to where they are in their buying decision-making process. Are they symptom-aware, problem-aware or solution-aware?

When all you are doing is speaking about your product, you are speaking to a small pond of people who are already *solution-aware* and are looking for the thing you're selling. This is a mistake that many new business owners make. You have, by nature of your marketing messages, shrunk your pool of potential buyers.

What you need to be doing is use your marketing to step back from your pond so you can widen it into a lake, and then into a sea. And we do this by speaking to people about their problems or their symptoms, who *don't know* yet that they need the product you are selling, because they haven't yet been diagnosed.

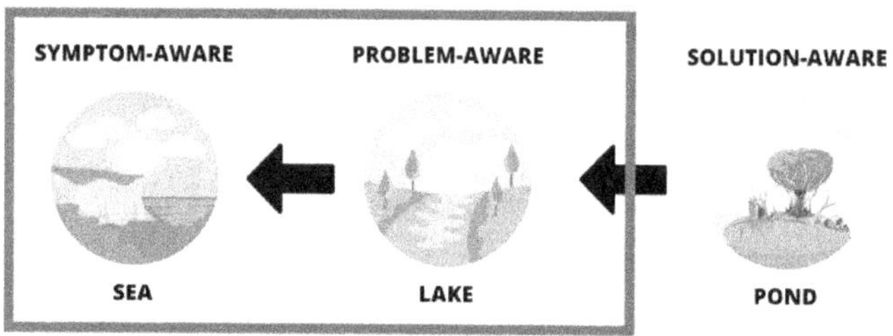

The most effective way we can get more leads is by using our marketing to instead speak to symptoms and problems.

This is what your lead magnet must do.

A lead magnet is an introductory offer that generates leads for your business. And by "leads", I mean emails. Because building your email list is going to be one of your most valuable assets in business. Building an email list means you will be future-proofing your business, because you won't be at the mercy of the platform's ever-changing algorithms and rules. You won't be at the mercy of an account shut-down or blocked ads.

Another term for a lead magnet is "irresistible offer." It's something so relevant to solve an acute problem or pain point that your audience cannot resist opting in. The purpose of a lead magnet is to turn a cold prospect into a curious one, or re-engage with existing customers. Lead magnets are easy to say yes to. Your potential customer lands on your page, immediately sees the value, and takes the action to get whatever you're offering. Some lead-magnets are free and others are paid.

We're going to take a look at some examples, but first, I'd like to give you a warning: do not get caught up in "what" a lead magnet is. No one's thinking to themselves, "Oh, I'd like to read a cheat sheet today." People think about how to achieve their goals. That's why mapping out your ideal buyer's before and after is so important. That's why understanding their symptoms are so important. So, don't get caught up in what it is, focus instead on *what it does* for them. Always have that in the back of your mind as you move forward.

COUPONS AND FREE SHIPPING

For those people who might already be solution-aware, coupons and free shipping are great lead magnets. Sometimes, your audience just needs a bit of a push to go ahead and buy your product. Discounts are a huge motivator because who doesn't love to save some money? Adding an introductory coupon for "first time purchasers," "survey takers' discount" or "new account sign-ups" can help you get their email or contact details and preferences to add to your database, while giving them a flat rate discount or a percentage-based discount coupon. Your coupon should be time-bound (offer ends in the next 48 hours) to increase the urgency for your target audience to take the desired action. You can also waive shipping charges to encourage visitors to complete your lead conversion. Free shipping of purchases over a certain amount will help you increase your sales volume. As far as lead magnets go, coupons and free shipping are foolproof ideas practiced at large.

GIVEAWAYS

Giveaways involve your brand gaining email addresses, followers, or engagements by giving away something of value to your audience (something they'll want!)

Giveaways is a great way to build your email database. You just need to promote the lead magnet (via the Traffic Pyramid we will be discussing) and send the traffic to a submission page where you will collect their email addresses for an entry into your giveaway.

Giveaways can also be an excellent method for you to get your existing followers to help boost your reach. All you have to do is ask them to follow your social media page, tag 3 to 5 like-minded friends, "like" and share your giveaway post on their feed or story. You can either reward the ones who have reeled in the newest interactions and followers, or use a random result generator app to pick winners fair and square.

While you give away samplers or hampers of your product, you also gain more leads! Everyone loves free stuff and prizes, especially if they win it!

QUIZZES

Self-discovery and curiosity are two evergreen desires. We love understanding ourselves better. Who isn't curious to know how we are unique from the others in the world? It's a powerful draw.

Quizzes help you provide valuable insights about your avatar's personality, skill sets, or custom solutions to problems they experience. Quizzes are engaging, personally compelling, enable you to understand your customers better and segment your list. They also offer high conversion rates, prepare your customers to buy from you, and are shareable. All of these have a great customer experience but are also good for targeted follow up based on what your audience answers.

We also come across a few e-commerce brands who are worth mentioning in regard to quizzes. *Rooted* is an e-commerce business that sells plants and accessories like DIY potting kits. They have an interesting quiz that matches your personality with the type of plant you may want to buy.

ThirdLove Lingerie's quiz tackles a huge pain point for women while de-risking shopping online for an item where fit is paramount. *Fenty Makeup* makes it super easy to find your shade which we used to happen only by visiting a beauty counter. *Y-Our Skin* is another one on the more detailed side because they actually create your unique formula for you. *Native* has a fast and fun scent quiz for their hero product, which is a deodorant. Also, when you finish the quiz, enter your name and email address, the digital mockup of the product has your name on it. It's absolutely brilliant.

CHECKLISTS, CHEATSHEETS, AND BLUEPRINTS

These three lead magnets make your potential customer's lives simpler. Providing a free checklist is a helping hand that shows your audience a path that will get them the results they desire. Checklists are the answer to *"I wish someone experienced told me what to do and how!"* These are simple guides that help people prepare to get a result. They're often fewer than 10 pages, too. Actually, some are only one page long! So, they're not complicated to create. Simply give your audience directions for solving a problem. You can use a checklist in all sorts of businesses. All you have to do is possess some knowledge and expertise over the domain you're addressing, and make life simpler for those who download your blueprint with precise pointers that mark their journey towards a goal (like taking back control of their lives by building a productive schedule). If you sell skincare products, you could offer a checklist on skin preparation. Perhaps a buying guide, or a comparison chart between the top competing products.

LIVE CONVERSION METHOD™:
EVENTS, TRUNK SHOWS & SUMMITS

The Live Conversion Method™ will revolutionize the way you grow your list, provide immense value for them, and tap into their desire for what you're selling. In the increasingly saturated markets we are operating in, the Live Conversion Method™ is one of the best ways to separate yourself from your competitors because you are able to show up for your audience and build an individual connection with them.

Now, what does it mean to show up for your audience? It ultimately means that you are present in the moment with them. They will have a truly VIP experience where they will feel seen and heard, where they get to ask their questions and get real, unfiltered answers and connect directly with the founder of the business.

You are going to use the Live Conversion Method™ to move your buyer through their decision-making process from being symptom-aware to problem-aware to solution-aware.

When they show up to your event, they will be dealing with the symptoms of a problem. No matter how big or small, you will be looking to help them with a plan to remove or ease this problem in their lives. This will form your lead magnet.

How this works: you invite your audience to participate in an event that you host live. It can be on any platform - Facebook, Instagram, YouTube, whichever – as long as you make it easy for them to show up. The event itself can be anywhere from 1 to 5 days. And they can be as short as 15 mins, or as long as 60 mins (depending on your content and how large the problem is you will be helping them with). Think of it like a live video series. In this event, you will be arming your audience with the mindset shift and skills they need to help them with the problem they have. And your product will naturally be the tool they need in order to get the result (the After) that they are looking for.

For example, one of our Growth Bosses, Susan, recently did a Live Conversion Method™ event in her Facebook Group. She used the event as a lead magnet, helping her audience through the process of creating a customized t-shirt for a loved one. She then sells that specific design on a t-shirt that she just helped her audience create. The event aims to establish a personal connection with the audience, and build lots of value before asking them to buy anything. Is that elegant, or what?

Another of our Growth Bosses, Danesa did a Live Conversion Method™ Trunk Show on her Facebook Page where she spoke about her vulnerabilities when she was a new mom and how thrifting and creating sparkle in her life with luxury vintage handbags and accessories helped her through that time. As she was speaking, she was also modeling her bags and accessories, going through them one-by-one. Sharing her experiences with other moms in her Live Conversion Method™ Trunk Show made her approachable and relatable and helped her build human connection with her audience.

Another client we worked with, Jess, did a 5-day Live Conversion Method™ event and really painted the picture for her audience each night. She was targeting a more diverse audience with her hot chocolate making machine and brought to life how her product can be used in people's different contexts... treating her partner, treating her children, treating herself... and she did over $23k that week!

Why were all the three so successful in gaining a substantial number of leads, and converting them into valuable customers? They all had one element in common - they met the audience at their respective comfort zones - their Before point - showed up for them, was present with them, answered their questions in real-time, showed their passion for the result they were helping their audience achieve – their After point - and bottom line... showed they cared. This is the most effective way to build human connection with your audience quickly and have them know, like and trust you. And ultimately, to want the product you are selling.

I will be going into a lot more detail about how to conduct a Live Conversion Method™ Event and Trunk Show in my second book. Just know for now that this is an incredibly effective lead magnet you can be leveraging.

Another way to leverage The Live Conversion Method™ is to conduct a Summit. A summit is one of the ultimate list-building strategies that focuses on leveraging other people's credibility, reputation and knowledge as your own way to magnetize leads. This is not the same as Influencer Marketing who have followers mainly on a social media platform (which we're going to get into later). The List Builders you are going to leverage are other business owners who have their own email databases, not just followers. Keep in mind that the fundamentals are the same - their audience should still be an audience who would be ideal for you.

The strategy is simple: get *at least* 5 List Builders together in non-competing (yet complementary) niches to co-promote a single event. Each List Builder contributes a section of content through a live interview with you for the summit and promotes the event to their list. So, if each of those five List Builders have 2,000 people on their list, that's a total pool of 10,000 potential attendees who could make it onto your own email list from this lead magnet!

KEY TAKEAWAYS:

1) A lead magnet is an introductory offer that is easy for your audience to opt in for. They're designed to turn a cold prospect (someone who doesn't know you) into a curious potential buyer.

2) When done right, your lead magnet can turn cold leads to converts. All you have to do is find what excites them the most. Effective lead magnets are: giveaways, quizzes, free shipping, discount coupons, checklists and cheat sheets and the Live Conversion Method™ Event, Trunk Show or Summit.

3) Focus on providing value and getting your audience hooked to your brand in a way that leaves them wanting more.

TAKE ACTION:

1. Choose an irresistible lead magnet that you think would work for your business.

2. Jot down the action that you want your audience to take using your lead magnet (refer to their before and after).

3. Create an engaging pitch for your audience that will capture their interest to participate and join your email list in exchange. Meaning, how would you communicate this offer to someone if you were speaking to them live? Remember: *make them an offer they cannot refuse.*

MASTER YOUR TRAFFIC PYRAMID

My head was in my hands as I looked at our bank account. I had to make the hard call; something, anything to stop the bleeding from continuing to happen. I should have known better. But there I was with our credit card bill in hand. Line after line read: "FACEBOOK…" We had racked up over $1200 in ad spend, without making any money. How was that possible?

I felt stupid, dumb, like a complete failure. How is it that we were making tens of thousands of dollars from ads for our clients, but we couldn't get it right for our own business?

Let me rewind a little and explain.

I had just moved to New York. My co-founder, Bona, and I had just decided to close up shop on the fashion-tech business we had been working on while we were still in Sydney. While we were trying to decide our next move, I bumped into an old friend of mine. We got to chatting. She told me she was moving her brick & mortar business online. Her business is a retail chocolate store. She knew my background growing The Choc Pot, and she invited me to help her with her online presence through digital marketing.

Bona and I worked on her account and were blown away with our results. Soon after, I started reaching out to some other boutiques and online businesses and we had a few clients on board who we were doing agency work for. And we were making them a ton of money! After a few months, we decided, "Why not start our own e-commerce business and we could make *even more* money?!"

We knew that with the success we'd already helped these other brands achieve, there was absolutely no way we could fail! Doing the same for ourselves as we were doing for our clients was going to be easy, we thought.

We dug out Bona's home-made skincare formulations, tweaked them, bottled them, and set up a website. Then we created some (in my opinion) pretty awesome ads!

I was struggling to contain my excitement because I couldn't wait to see the money rolling in! These ads were going to be the silver bullet to growth, sales and success! I couldn't wait! We turned them on and waited.

Ok… nothing yet… that's fine, we just need to give it a few days so that the algorithm can learn… Still nothing. Ok? We tweaked our creative (text and images) so we could grab people's attention. We got some new followers on our page, but no sales!? We changed our copy, had some click through to our website, *but still, no sales*. What was going on!? We looked at everything. We were doing this successfully for all these other brands. Why wasn't it working for ours? We were tweaking our ads until we no longer had any more money to test with. After wasting all this money on ads and not getting many sales, we turned them off and tried to work out what was going on.

And then it hit me.

When we compared the performance of our business with the brands we were working with. The one obvious thing that stood out was that those brands already had an audience. *They already had customers.* They had put some time and effort into getting a pool of buyers without the ads. And only now were they reinvesting into ads with a proven audience. And we hadn't done that yet. That was the step we had completely missed.

By that point, we had no more money to spend on ads and I had to figure out another way. In my desperation, I started finding individuals on social media I thought would be absolutely ideal buyers of ours. I reached out to them individually through my social media accounts, having conversations with them to find out what was working for them and what wasn't. Before I knew it, we had people buying! I was making sales, and I wasn't even spending any money on ads! I knew then that I had cracked a code, yet didn't quite know how to articulate it. Then, something magical happened… in the shower.

For whatever strange reason, I get my best ideas in the shower. Too much information? Sorry, but it's true! Showers are actually a creative marketing strategy at *Growth Boss*. :).

One morning, I was holding a marketing strategy session (aka taking a shower) and I was thinking about the day ahead. That day, I was hosting our *3-day Cold to Converted Challenge*, and something was bothering me, but I couldn't pinpoint what it was. You know that feeling, where you've been working on something for a long time and it's good enough. Yet, your intuition tells you that you're only a little tweak away from turning that into something *great*!? It was one of those moments.

When I asked the question about what our group was currently doing to get traffic to their websites, everyone across the map said "I'm on Instagram and Facebook." Then, as I prodded some more, a few others said "Oh yeah, I also work with some Influencers on Instagram." Then an even smaller subset said, "I've also tried Facebook ads but they just don't work." Then I had a massive *aha moment.*

These conversations were highlighting a traffic *pyramid;* a progression of tiers, or *phases*. These are specific marketing activities e-commerce owners do in order to master their traffic. These tiers are sequential. Meaning: in most cases, you'll move up the pyramid in step-by-step order. Yet, it is also cyclical. As in: when you're mastering a different channel (like going from

Facebook to Instagram) you can move between each tier, depending on what you want for your situation. This is what we want to be doing as we build out our traffic machine. If you follow the strategy I'm about to lay out, you can build your own audience of ideal buyers without spending any money on ads first. That way, you can cost-effectively scale when you are ready to invest in ads.

I'm going to show you a step-by-step process for gaining a tremendous amount of market research that you can apply to your advertising. The best part is: you'll be making money as you learn, as opposed to spending money to learn. You'll be testing and iterating your brand personality and the types of content that resonate. You'll be leveraging other people's audiences and track which influencers drive the most qualitied traffic to your website or social media accounts. You'll know how to analyze your results. Here it is…

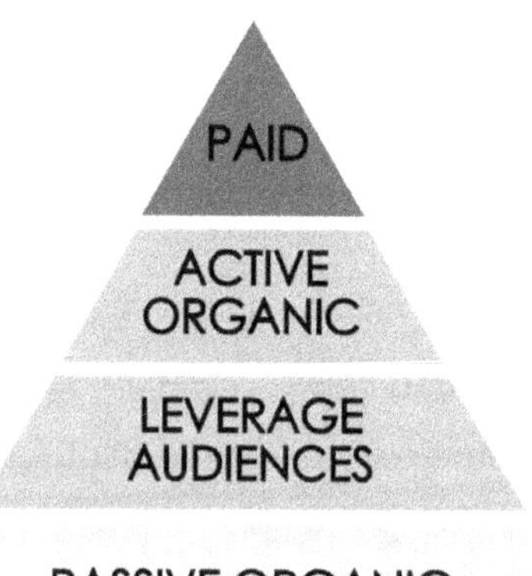

PASSIVE ORGANIC

Passive Organic Marketing. This is the first tier. If you're "just on" any one of the major platforms, you're doing Passive Organic Marketing. Also, it's not *passive* in the sense that you're not doing anything. You may be consistently posting material on Facebook for instance, which is hardly sitting back and doing nothing. That's real work. What I mean by the word *passive* is that you're waiting for your customer to stumble upon you. When they do, it's a *reactive* customer. It's not something you can directly measure, like an advertising campaign, for instance. One of the best parts of Passive Organic Marketing is that you're developing your voice, gaining insights into how the platform functions, and what all of its features are. You're also developing a portfolio of content for people to snoop through when they arrive on your profile or page.

Leveraging other people's audiences. This is where you are collaborating with someone else who has a large audience that you're tapping into, and drawing that audience back into your world. One part of it is what we might commonly refer to as *Influencer Marketing*, however as I'll expand upon, there are a host of other types of people (like List Builders), audiences, and ways you can be leveraging!

The bottom line is that here, you are entering into the influencer's world. Sometimes that's doing a co-hosted live, having the Influencer or List Builder send out an email, a shout-out, or sharing your videos/content in some capacity. It doesn't matter what platform they're on, as long as they are sending that traffic back to you and your lead magnet.

One of the things you should understand before getting into influencer marketing is this: it is a volume game. A single reference is likely not going to transform your business overnight. With a large enough group of Influencers or List Builders, however, their powers combined create an almost compound interest effect on your exposure. Your potential buyers start thinking, "Why is this person showing up everywhere?" And it's because you've gotten crystal clear on the types of Influencers and List Builders you want associated with your brand, that have the right audience for you, and you have created these connections with the Influencers and List Builders.

Active Organic Marketing. As a quick summary, *active organic* is an individual outreach and community-building strategy. You're building your audience at an *individual* level and cultivating relationships with them. This strategy in itself could be a profit center in your business. Meaning, you can set up a daily habit (or standard operating system if you have a marketing team), and use this strategy to sell your products.

Paid Ads. You've done the hard work. You've organically built your audience of ideal buyers and you can now reinvest into paid advertising to really scale. Having said that, paid ads are a whole new ball game that need a strategy of their own as well as some time and money for experimentation. The key is to be strategic with this testing, use the data to learn more about your audience and optimize your ads accordingly.

Next, we're going to break down each phase of the *Traffic Pyramid.* Please go through these in the order we present them. Think of this like an investment portfolio that attracts compound interest.

PHASE 1:
PASSIVE ORGANIC MARKETING

My friend, Yen, and I were both in our second year of university working on an entrepreneurship competition (talk about being a nerd, right?). It was the middle of summer, and we were at Yen's house with four other people. The plan was that all six of us would hop in the pool, because we had to stay cool to be productive, naturally. Then, we would get on with the rest of the assignment.

As we were bobbing in the water, we somehow got to talking about this new thing called "Facebook." Yen had just been recently invited. It really was back in the OG days when you had to be in university/college and actually be invited to be able to set up an account. Everyone was clamoring for an invite!

No one really knew what it was, but the exclusivity had massive appeal.

After signing up, it was a bit of fun finding other people on there from high school, "friend requesting" them, posting all the photos and doing the tagging thing… and then I lost interest.

It was only a few short years, and many iterations of Facebook later, I had started my first business that I recalled the updated functionality of being able to start a business page.

I knew the basics of how the platform worked and I'd actually accumulated quite a few friends on there, so I started the business page and invited all of my friends to like it.

Unbeknownst to me, that would be my first foray into some form of viral marketing. Because from there, my friends invited their friends to like it, and it grew organically from there. We didn't even have great content. It was all completely passive organic marketing but we had ridden the growth wave of Facebook. Mind blown emoji!

A few months later, Anne, one of our casual staff members, who was still in high school asked me if we were on Instagram. I had NO IDEA what she was talking about. It was one of those few times that I felt incredibly old as a young person. So, she grabbed my phone, and set The Choc Pot up with a profile. The photos were ugggly! But we were on there and her instructions were, "Just keep posting photos.'' So, we did. To this day, I still credit Instagram as one of the main reasons we were able to grow quickly. We had people come to our little store from the other side of Sydney mentioning that they found out about us through Instagram. It was insane! All we were doing was posting photos (passive organic marketing) but we had ridden the growth wave of Instagram.

For some reason I've been fortunate enough to ride the growth wave of two of the biggest social media platforms with my first business. Completely passively and organically. I thought it would be the same with my second, and third, and fourth business. But let me tell you: it hasn't.

I have struggled since then to be able to post something and get the types of reach, likes, follows, and engagement I had easily with my first business. We have to realize: as platforms grow and evolve and search for monetization, our ability to reach a large audience organically will change and shrink as per their algorithms. Now, we have to be intentional with how we utilize these platforms, and be open to shifting with the platform as they do. More importantly, we have to be intentional with the outcome that we are looking to get from these platforms. As time has gone on, I've borne witness to many friends, acquaintances and other business owners have pages shut down, ads accounts shut down, be told what they can and can't post. What this has been highlighting is the risk in putting all our eggs into the social media basket. For example, if Instagram is your main way of getting traffic and your account gets shut down… where is that going to leave you and your business? How will you be able to continue making sales? Let's be intentional with what outcome we are looking to get from these platforms. And that outcome? It is going to be to build your email list. Because your email list will always be something that you own.

Whichever platforms you decide to be on, you need to think strategically about how you are going to use the lead magnets we discussed in the previous chapter to funnel your audience onto your email list.

WHERE SHOULD YOU BE?

The fundamental concept of which platforms you should be on hinges on where your audience is. Ensure that you are strategic about the platforms you tackle first. I know how overwhelming it can be to try to keep up with all the different social media platforms out there, and the new ones that keep popping up. One of the common scenarios with e-commerce owners and social media is they're spread too thin. They're trying to on all channels at the same time. They're going a mile wide as opposed to deep. This is routed in the misconception there is a single, one-size-fits-all, traffic plan. Yet there isn't. There is no "single solution" to a channel. It is a discovery process for you as a brand, and who your customers are.

There are two types of Passive Organic Marketing platform strategies: creating demand, and meeting demand. Let's take a deeper dive into each one.

PLATFORMS THAT CREATE DEMAND

Platforms that create demand are first and foremost a "discovery" platform. Meaning, they are about providing entertainment, news, or a place where people might stumble upon something fascinating. Demand creating platforms are based on having scroll-stopping content. An interesting image or copy grabs the attention of the viewer into their curiosity phase. These are platforms where viewers find your content, love and validate it, and demand more of it. You can use your lead magnet as bait with awesome creative and copy to cast it into this pool to gather leads.

Facebook. It's a beast of a platform. No secret. Statistics show that 85% all of orders from social media sites come from Facebook, which means it is one of the best places for you to start with. Facebook works out so efficiently for businesses because almost everyone (and their dogs) are on there. Facebook also has its own "Marketplace," which is great for ecommerce owners and brands to showcase products. Their location filters help you target local audiences easily, just like Google's local ratings. So yes, Facebook makes sense to be on. But the question is "how"? Because if you already have a business page on there, you may have noticed the reach of any of your posts being abysmal! This is because… even if you did everything right… the *maximum* reach you might have with a post is 2%. As I said, abysmal. At the time of writing this, my suggestion is that if you want to be effective on Facebook, you need to create and manage your own group. Creating communities is the vision for Facebook, and so if we want to be successful on the platform, we also need to align to that vision.

Instagram, too. It's also up there as a favorite because it's all image-based. The platform is teeming with hashtags, polls, reels and lives you can use to draw out more followers. With its e-commerce features of "Tap to shop" and "Checkout", Instagram is helping entrepreneurs drive more traffic and generate better sales. A Facebook report shows how 87 percent of users take action after viewing product information on Instagram, and 46 percent of these had made a purchase.

TikTok. The world has been taken by storm with the presence of TikTok. The platform attracts brands to collaborate with social media celebrities, playing a vital role in the influencer culture. In just 15 to 30 seconds per video, brands have the perfect endorsements that sell their products. It's also a great platform to try your hand at "going viral" when you don't have a large following.

A few insights about these platforms:

- People don't generally go on these platforms to search for something. They go on these platforms to explore and scroll.

- They don't have a specific intent, they're just trying to discover, be entertained, and feel connected.

- On these platforms, you're not really meeting demand, you're creating demand by ensuring you have great scroll-stopping content, and a feed that is going to captivate your audience and have them want to stay and learn more about you and what you do.

- The people who are on these platforms are generally symptom-aware, and not yet problem-aware or solution-aware.

- Your job on these platforms is to help to move people from just being symptom-aware, to becoming problem-aware and solution-aware, so that they ultimately buy from you.

PLATFORMS THAT MEET DEMAND

Platforms that meet demand essentially mean that you use them to find something. They're search-based platforms people visit with an intention. They type something in to get some type of result. They're result-oriented, which is why demand-meeting platforms are based on the keyword or search engine optimization (SEO) strategy. Here, you use your lead magnet as bait (with the right keywords) to hook your audience that are already looking for something to help them with a symptom they're feeling, a problem they know they have, or for a particular solution.

Which platforms are demand-meeting?

Pinterest. Pinterest is great for e-commerce because it is based on keyword image searches. It allows users to find products, images, quotes, and anything that can be represented by an image. One of the great things about Pinterest is that you can have private and public "pin up boards" of your own, where you can save pictures you like, and categorize them as per your agenda. Pinterest keeps track of your search preferences or favorite concepts using your pin board, and suggests users with more content that leads to articles, blogs, websites, e-commerce sites or lead magnets. People can view your public pins and save them which increases your visibility.

YouTube. YouTube is one of those platforms that can't be replaced because they are the go-to for every person when it comes to tutorials, entertainment, and documentaries. Content creators get to monetize their channels and videos, giving them an alternative source of income over direct product selling. But the main money-making appeal isn't in front-end monetization (meaning, getting paid per video view, etc.) The real money is in creating content people love, and then directing the audience to your lead magnet.

Google. Do we even need to explain the magnitude of impact this search engine has created since its inception? I'll keep it short and simply say: if what you're searching for exists, you will find it on Google. Their SEO and page ranking dictates how businesses curate content and run their websites. Ranking high on Google's results page means you're the business it would suggest when the audience searches for something related to your brand.

Some insights with platforms that meet demand:

- Generally, search-based is where people are using the platform with an intention. They are there to search something. They're putting in a search term with the intent of learning more about it, trying to find a solution.
- At this stage, the people who are searching are generally already problem-aware or solution-aware

Choosing a platform that fits your traffic pyramid

One of the common challenges we've noticed with many e-commerce entrepreneurs is that they are trying to be everywhere, on all social media platforms, creating much less valuable content because their attention is divided. This leads them to not giving enough time to a single channel's audience, unable to establish a bond and hence ending up with less followers or conversions. Going a mile wide rather than a mile deep won't lead them to the gold. If you stick to surface level activity, you're going to get surface level expertise. I always recommend picking one 'create demand' and one 'meet demand' channel first and sticking with those so you can "go deep" into those two verticals first. Here's why sticking to a maximum of two platforms at any one time and exhausting all of its verticals is better than going into several boats at once:

- You can get more done without any distractions.
- You will feel more in control of your marketing and less overwhelmed juggling too many accounts.
- It will give you room to improve your only business account rather than maintaining several haphazard ones.
- It will enable you to build routine behaviors in operations once you understand the peak interaction times and audience's behavior.

If you want to have a presence on all platforms with the same intensity and engagement, you need to master one platform before you move to another. All platforms are social networking channels, yet different in their user behavior, search engine optimization parameters and how they amplify a brand's content. Being all over the place will not just overwhelm you, it can also set your progress back because you'd be distributing your attention and time between multiple channels.

CREATING CONTENT TO CONVERT

I have a free Facebook community of female e-commerce entrepreneurs, called E-Commerce Growth Secrets, where I conduct free weekly live training and real-time audits (on everything from websites, to emails, to Instagram accounts).

As we are getting Instagram account audit requests, I was hearing the exact same thing time and time again… "Deirdre, I can't get any of my Instagram followers to buy!", "No one is converting!", "I'm posting all the time but still no sales!"

It's a common frustration, and also a common misconception. Yes, our social media channels are meant to help us sell. But also, no, our social media channels are not meant to help us sell. I know, it's mind boggling, right? Here's what I mean…

As we went through and conducted these audits in our group; I noticed the same thing over and over again. This is the common mistake (probably) 95% of business owners make: *only posting about our product!* Post after post, as I scroll down these feeds, all I see are photos of product. On a wooden table, with a white background, in a garden… same product, different backgrounds. Over and over again.

Something we should keep in mind is that as humans, we all like to buy things. But we hate being sold to. Even though we know this intuitively, why do we still insist on only trying to sell?

I'm going to be diving deep into exactly what content to create and how to create it in my third book, but in the meantime, I wanted to explain how I think about creating content on social media.

And this comes back to what people are using these platforms for and where they are in the buying decision-making process. When you only create content about your product, you are assuming that your audience all want or need what you have. Which means that you have shrunk your pool of potential buyers into a pond – to people who are only solution-aware. They are looking for the thing you're selling.

What you need to do is to mix your content so that you are also speaking to people who are problem-aware (you're widening your pond into a lake), and symptom-aware (you're widening your lake into a sea).

 How this looks in reality is that you are going to be rotating your content to speak to the different people in your audience: meeting them where they are. Not all of your call-to-actions are going to be "buy now." Because again, then you'll only be speaking to people who are solution-aware.

For people who are symptom-aware, it might be using content that speaks to exactly what they might be saying, thinking and feeling right now, at their Before point. Your aim is to have them realize what the underlying cause or problem is for this so that they now become problem-aware. Your call-to-action on this content might be to a lead magnet, such as a quiz, that goes into more detail about this "problem" while "diagnosing" them.

For people who are problem-aware, your content will focus on having them realize that it is quick, simple and easy for them to solve it. Make it a no-brainer! This could look like how-to's or quick guides, with the call-to-action to opt-in for a lead magnet that goes into detail on the "how-to".

Weaved into all your content is how your product is going to be integral in helping them achieve the result they are looking for. For example, it forms part of your "how-to" steps, or it might be an end point on your quiz.

Your content does not need to be used to sell all the time. It just needs to naturally lead them into the next step, which more likely than not, will be to opt-in for your lead magnet. Once they're on your email database, you can then nurture them into the sale. More on this in my second book!

Once you've decided upon the platform that works best for you and the type of content you should be creating, you need to grab the attention of the audience. A part of finding your ideal customer is to leverage other people's audiences, with the aim of making their audience yours!

PHASE 2: LEVERAGING OTHER PEOPLE'S AUDIENCES

Leveraging other people's audiences is super powerful for many reasons: it's incredibly effective to help you amplify your message *quickly*; it gets you more visibility and awareness; it gives your brand credibility; it helps you grow your own follower-base and email list; and it can help you fast-track sales growth.

Because of all of these reasons, I am a HUGE fan of this strategy. But only when it's done right with the requisite thought put into it.

I know it might be tempting to go out there and start to find all these people with large audiences to work with, but you need to consider who to work with, how to work with them, and ultimately, what is the outcome you are looking for?

Are you looking for direct sales? Are you looking to increase brand awareness and visibility? Are you looking to build your followers and/or email database?

Being clear on the direct outcome you are looking to achieve with leveraging someone else's audiences will make it easier to communicate, help them funnel their audience to the right place and ultimately, to track.

There are two groups of people we can look to tap into when looking to leverage an audience. They are (1) Influencers and (2) List Builders.

Influencers are how we might typically think about influencer marketing. They are individuals or accounts on any given platform who have followers (e.g. Instagram, Facebook, TikTok) or subscribers (e.g. YouTube, podcasts) where they generally can't get *directly* in touch with them unless they pop up on their audience's explore or home feed, or the platform sends a notification about new content.

List Builders are people or businesses who typically have an email list that they can directly reach out to. Yes, there may be promotion or spam filters, but typically with a good enough hook, the email will get opened.

Let's dive first into how we might work with Influencers.

INFLUENCER MARKETING

There are two types of influencers to consider when you're doing Influencer Marketing: the platform owners, and the people who've mastered the platform and have audiences.

You can think of this like a big digital party. The host of the party provides the space, the vibe, the games, and tools for all the guests to attend and have a good time. The guests join the party and have a blast, because they're able to interact with all sorts of people they may not have been able to meet if they didn't show up.

The analogy really works because all parties are different. Some play house music. Other's play hip-hop, or alternative, or rock n' roll. Depending on the vibe of the party, you'll have different types of people who show up. Some guests make fools of themselves because they're self-consumed and obnoxious. Other people are the life of the party; they're special guests, because they make the party an enjoyable experience, even dragging introverts like me out of our shells. They're the real facilitators of fun, corralling new people into the social circle and stimulating conversations. Their enthusiasm is infectious. Plus: *they are faithful ambassadors of the host*, endorsing them at every opportunity for the party.

We want to align ourselves with both the host (the owner of the platform), and those special guests with their own circles (influencers who've effectively built an audience on those platforms).

By aligning with the host, I don't mean *become friends with Mark Zuckerberg.* I mean: aligning with the host's rules and best-practices for a good user experience. In other words, you want to *think like the platform owner* and make the party better for everyone. If you were in Zuckerberg's position with Facebook, what would you do to keep your platform at the top of the ranks, exciting for people to stay there and useful enough that all businesses joined the party too? That's how you keep the guests engaged and having a good time. As the platform becomes more saturated and "boring," you'll need to find more and better ways to keep people having a great time.

How did The Zuck do that? One answer is: by going all in on communities. Their bet is that people being social creatures will want to form and stay engaged in communities, so he brought together people who have similar interests - for example, people who love buying organic products - led by the life of their party (an influencer), and organic business owners found an excellent event to network with such interested buyers.

Like sororities and frat parties, Facebook Groups bring people with common interests together so people get to socialize better. That's why Facebook Groups took off, and the reach of group posts is much higher than a post on a Facebook page. They bring businesses and people together. How has

Instagram done this? By continuing to add to short and entertaining content. From posts, stories, Instagram Live and IGTV, to reels, they have covered their bases.

What is your lesson here when I ask you to think like the platform owner? Once you choose a platform, you have to be as visible to the audience as possible, which means throwing a banquet with a bit of everything - images, videos, live sessions, reels or stories. And yes, while you can certainly build a decent following and hold a great party doing this on your own, if you want to fast-track your follower growth, you'll need influencers.

Take a look at Krystal Bick, the New York City based fashion and travel influencer. A self-proclaimed cinephile, she uses stunning visual storytelling to inspire her hundreds of thousands of followers to romanticize their day-to-day lives. Whether it be a luxury candle burning in her West Village apartment or a unique silk face mask elevating her Sunday brunch outfit, Krystal partners with select brands to bring their products to life in an aspirational but attainable way for her audience. There are many such influencers for every niche who could feature your business as a collaboration or endorsement. Let me tell you about an example of how I leveraged this strategy…

LEVERAGING INFLUENCE

I knew just how good our desserts were. We had put so much effort into creating these divine creations and had so many taste-testing parties, that it was almost an impossibility to not be successful. When we opened The Choc Pot, I was expecting our doors to be beaten down. I was naive though. I believed our dishes alone were good enough to have people finding us and flooding the store. Two months into opening, reality struck. I had to get real about what we were doing because we were only making $100, maybe $200 a day. Some days went by only selling a handful of coffees! We were bleeding money because we had rent and wages to pay; we had supplier bills piling up!

The "build it and they will come" strategy was not working! It was one of the loneliest moments in my life, to the point where I started feeling claustrophobic being in the store. And I knew that I had to do something differently. I had to work out some way of getting the word out there. Because even through all of my doubts, uncertainty, crippling anxiety, and the feeling that for some reason, people just didn't like us – there was a fire inside me that knew we were onto something.

Fast forward a few weeks later, my husband and I had one of those very rare nights that we were both able to take a breather. At our dinner date we received a call from one of our *very frantic* team members, saying, "Guys you have to come in. I can't explain right now, I have to serve this drink. But we need help! You've gotta come in… Now!!" We couldn't help thinking "OMG! What's going on? Has something blown up? Have we lost power? What is it?"

So, we ran to the car, hopped in, and drove as quickly as we could (without running any red lights), trying not to freak out. When we got to the front of the store, I could still remember the sight before me. *The place was packed!*

We had a line of people waiting to get tables! We had people moving tables to create more space. Our poor team members were literally running back and forth from the kitchen to the tables serving people. It was chaos, but glorious chaos. It felt like we had become an overnight success.

What had we done that changed our downward spiral?

I had reached out to a bunch of different bloggers and influencers. They were coming in, maybe one or two a week, for a few weeks. It's not like getting them to post or blog about us made us an immediate overnight success, but it was the momentum they were building. The more that people saw us, read about us, the more that they were like, "Okay, I have to try this place because *EVERYONE* is talking about them!"

And I had an "aha!" moment. The ONLY way we could build this type of momentum quickly is to leverage people with large audiences, where their audience is an ideal fit with ours. That's what we're going to be exploring next…

FIND YOUR INFLUENCERS

How could you reach 10,000 of your ideal customers? You could reach out individually, but that would take a lot of time. If you were sending 100 PM's per day, you could do that in less than a third of a year. Or, you could work with 5 influencers who each have 2,000 people as an audience and have it done by next Friday. See how that simplifies everything!?

Influencers have built their audience. If they've done it in the correct way, their audience trusts them, engages with their posts, and (most importantly) takes that action the influencer asks them to take.

Leveraging influencer's audiences is "win-win-win." The audience gets to know you and your products, which gives them the results they want. The influencer gets the social currency of being "in the know." And you get to add to your email database or even make sales!

There are a variety of ways you could be working with influencers. One is that you can leverage them to directly sell your product to their audience. However, if you only have this outcome in mind, you may be setting yourself up for disappointment.

The second way (and increasingly becoming my favorite way), is collaborating with them with the intention of adding to your email list. Which means that you would be creating a lead magnet with the influencer to promote to their audience.

I like this route because you are continuing to build your number one asset in your business – your email database. And then you can use your time to continue building a relationship with them via email!

It's important to mention that when looking to work with Influencers on social media: there's a lifecycle. At first, we like to target "micro influencers" who are people with approx. 100K followers or fewer. We're looking for people who want to grow with us. Usually before the 100K level, the influencer is not necessarily looking for upfront payment for shout-outs or post shares.

Pay attention to the number of followers they have, and the engagement rates on their page. These days it's simple to buy followers, which ultimately flops, because you'll see 25K followers with barely 250 likes and annoying bot comments. The point of this is to track down genuine influencers and build relationships with them. You do this by reaching out to them on their business accounts or email to send them a freebie sample package of your product or invite them to your cafe, like we did! Inviting similar business owners or collaborating with them on podcast interviews or lives is a great way to join forces and have their audience check you out. The same goes for guest blogging, where you write for their platform (usually for free unless you're already famous) to reach their audience.

Before reaching out to an influencer, you want to go for quality over quantity. We're not looking for someone with five million unengaged followers. We want people who have a list of loyal and engaged fans. Also, we want an influencer who knows how to promote – whether it is your product or your lead magnet. Now that you've found them, how exactly do you work with them?

WORKING WITH INFLUENCERS

When we first leveraged influencer marketing for The Choc Pot, I have to admit that I didn't really know what I was doing. There was no real strategy to exactly who we were reaching out to and how we would be working with them. At the time, we were fortunate that as the platform was growing, people were organically growing with them, which meant that not only did they have a true follower base, but they also didn't have huge expectations or demands.

That isn't the case any longer. We now need to work with them in a way that not only adds value to ourselves, but also adds value to them and their followers. They've built an asset in their follower base, and it is in their best interest to protect it from content that is not relevant or of value.

When I was thinking about what more we could do with them for The Choc Pot, having worked with them for a period of time and seeing how they were working with other brands in retail and e-commerce, I started noticing a trend.

Giving them the ability to put their name to something - to collaborate with brands on something that was unique to them - gave them an opportunity to really promote something one-of-a-kind that was valuable to them and their followers.

And so, for The Choc Pot, we started collaborating with them on new desserts that they had direct input into. They would come up with the flavor combinations and perhaps a rough sketch or provide visual inspiration for what they were thinking, and we would bring it to life for them.

And they promoted the heck out of it!

Now, I am definitely not suggesting that you create new products with influencers (especially if you're just starting out), but how do you take that concept and apply it to something less labor-intensive and helps you build your traffic? How can you collaborate with them on a lead magnet? Perhaps a giveaway? A quiz? Be creative and have some fun with it! And definitely get their input! The more that they can co-create with you, the more bought-in they will become to actually promote you and the offer. You've made it irresistible for them!

You can find influencers on all social media platforms. We can also expand the definition of influencers to anyone with a *network*. Meaning, they don't have to just be influencers on social media.

They may also be List Builders…

LIST BUILDERS

I want to make this clear because being in e-commerce, I know it is tempting to think about this one-dimensionally - to leverage influencers in the way we know - those on social media. However, we know now that if we are building up our email database asset, there are a host of other people's audiences we can be leveraging, who I call List Builders. List Builders are people who have and are building their own email list.

Collaborating with other businesses is one of the best ways to do this. One of my Growth Bosses, Susan, will be collaborating on a Live Conversion Method™ summit with therapists in her area who have the same audience she is targeting for her Hidden Power Hoodies. Another one of my Growth Bosses, Anu, has been writing guest articles for magazines in her local area. Again, with the same target market as hers. Another of my Growth Bosses, Liuba, who sells skincare products is helping women holistically with their health and could collaborate with dance instructors and yoga teachers.

In fact, very simply, you could even start by collaborating with other e-commerce businesses to hold a Live Conversion Method™ Trunk Show. There are so many exciting possibilities to collaborate with List Builders. You can only be capped by your imagination!

It can be daunting to find and reach out to potential Influencers and List Builders to work with, which is why it is important to think about what value you can add to them to help them grow with you.

Keep in mind, there is no such thing as an overnight success. The influencer & list builder strategy, like any effective marketing method, is based on consistent effort and momentum. Influencers love posting great content on their page, and yours could be the next post they make. List Builders love to email their database with something valuable to themselves and their list. Work with influencers & list builders that have an audience that fit your ideal customer base, who might love your products or your lead magnets and give it a try, increasing your audience base in turn.

PHASE 3:
ACTIVE ORGANIC MARKETING

We've all heard the all-too common experience new ecommerce owners have with paid ads. The story goes: "I invested $3,000 for ads that literally did nothing!" (and as you know now, I totally get it!). From that point forward, they're gun-shy because they don't want to repeat the same mistakes.

We've run into these types of situations frequently. When we do a diagnostic review of a business owners' campaigns, it becomes clear they didn't have the ammunition necessary before they started running ads that could find the right audience, land the right messaging and produce a profit. The cause of this type of situation is a matter of preparation. Active Organic Marketing is one of the most powerful ways for you to discover your audience, marketing messages, offers, and creative. It's a real boots-on-the-ground mentality. You build your audience, sell your products, and compile all the material that helped get those results so you can leverage those assets in your paid strategy if you should decide to go ahead with that.

Remember Bernie Sander's mittens that blew up so much, the teacher who made them could not take any more orders? That could be you, without a random stroke of luck turning your product into a meme. Here, you will learn exactly how to make your product take off with a strategy and the intention for growth. So… where do you begin?

Always start on the 'create demand' platform you are focusing your Passive Organic Marketing activities on. Did you choose Instagram or Facebook?

From there, you want to find your audience. If you've chosen to focus on Instagram, you are going to do that by looking at the hashtags your ideal buyer might be using, or looking through the followers of other businesses or accounts you believe they are currently congregating with.

If you've chosen Facebook, you are going to find your audience by finding the groups that they would be members of.

You now know my story about losing thousands of dollars jumping straight into running Facebook ads. Unfortunately, it's a very common story for new e-commerce business owners. Which is why I cannot stress enough how important this tier of the traffic pyramid is. When you know your ideal buyer as you would a family member, you know their interests and behaviors, and you know how they talk about their pain point or their goals. That's when it's almost like you have your ad audience built *and* ad copy written for you!

I felt like a proud mother-hen after speaking to one of my Growth Bosses recently. Bo Zhao had become a member of

Growth Boss Academy to get help growing her baby gear rental business (like Rent the Runway but for baby gear).

I remember the slight frustration in her voice just before she joined the Academy. Like many new business owners, she knew she was onto something, but hadn't quite been able to get the traction she needed to validate this new business model.

She knew this was going to be the business that would be able to help mothers all around the world reduce the stress, money and waste that comes with buying and growing out of baby gear.

The problem was that while there were many women she had spoken to and sought feedback from previously saying "yes, love this idea!", "Yes, this is a great idea!", "the world totally needs this!" They weren't signing up. *Even when she was offering it to them for free!*

That left her wondering: was this really such a great idea? All these women are so generous with their time, and when given the opportunity to be a tester with no cost, they didn't take it? If that wasn't working, what else would?

She tested some other ways. She tried holding webinars, providing training about the things you really need as a new mom, with a lead in to her pitch. Still crickets. She even tried running some Black Friday holiday deals with a 50% off discount. Still nothing. She then tried running some ads which got her a lot of spam responses and one slightly legitimate one who turned out was just "bored" when she came across Bo's ad and wanted to tell her that it sounded like a great idea.

Nothing was working!

And Bo, who had an Ivy League MBA, was left wondering if maybe the business wasn't as great an idea as she thought… or that maybe it was just her. All she wanted to do was to help other moms out there with this problem that she struggled with, but no one was compelled in the same way to try it.

And then she joined Growth Boss Academy, and now armed with the right outreach strategy, she joined more targeted Facebook groups. She wasn't limiting herself to the one Philadelphia Mom group she had been nurturing before. She started joining groups related to "sustainable living," "sustainable moms," "sustainable Philly," "evidence-based parenting," etc.

Then she started having conversations and going through the "2 weeks of pain." It's the period of time that is super awkward and makes you feel self-conscious because you have no idea what you're doing at first. She literally would blurt out everything about her business in one message initially. Yes, it was painful and awkward. All the things you feel when you're learning something new. I remember speaking to her during those two weeks and I could sense the uncertainty. She'd ask me, "How long is this supposed to take? How much time am I supposed to spend on this? When will I see results?"

I knew that this was going to be the pivotal moment because this is the point when most people give up. They would rationalize it in other ways like, "Well my product isn't worth a lot, should I be spending all this time trying to get these handful of sales in this way?" And then they'll just go back to doing things the "safe" way. But what they forget is that people buy from people first. They want to know who you are and what you stand for, especially if you haven't built up your brand yet. This was what Bo also realized. Because now she was having the right conversations with the right people.

Finally, we started getting bombarded (in a great way!) with daily posts and texts from her about a new sale she had, new customers started rolling in. It made a massive difference to her business. She was on a roll. She told me: "it feels awesome. It feels so natural now. It literally feels like a normal conversation I get to have to help someone."

REACHING OUT, MINUS THE AWKWARD SLIME

When reaching out to strangers, the last thing you'd want is to have an awkward undertone of copy/paste spam and that dreadful anti-personal "slime" that makes them roll their eyes and hit the delete button. The first outreach is to initiate a real conversation with them, and find out what they'd be looking for help with in aspects relevant to your product. Go for rapport. Think about how you could genuinely get to know the person and what makes them tick. The key word is *discovery.* You reach out knowing your strategy, yet with a real desire to discover who's an appropriate fit for your tribe, email list, and offers. Awkward slime is allergic to authenticity. It loves when people have counter-intentions and are emotionally hung up on outcomes. So, steal the slime's nutrition: be authentic with your outreach, and talk to people as if you would in a cafe, or face-to-face at a networking event.

Also, respect your time, of course. That's where pre-qualification comes into play. You want to build your audience with people who are a right fit. If you've followed the steps in the "Identify Your Audience" section, you should have a clear filter around who gets your time, and who doesn't. Have a look at the profile of the person you're about to message and take stock. You don't have to creep on their life history. But find something that stands out to you as a conversation starter; something you could address. Move the conversation into the DMs. Thank them for connecting/accepting your friend/follow request. End your interactions with a question to help you get to know them better.

For example: *"Hey, Abby! Thank you for accepting my friend request. I checked out your profile, and saw these beautiful dogs on your feed. What breed are they?"*

Give a little bit of information about yourself by responding to their reply, and ask a question at the end, slowly transitioning into questions regarding your business niche. Have a natural conversation. If you're both comfortable, you could even send them voice notes or exchange pictures of common interests from time to time to establish a more personal bond. Sometimes, you message the wrong person, and that's okay too. It's better to realize you're barking up the wrong tree rather than waste time forcing a conversation. How do you figure that out? It's simple. You'll feel like you're pulling teeth… *"if it doesn't flow, let it go."*

I've noticed that people fear doing outreach because they don't want to be pushy. So, the other thing to keep in mind is that every interaction achieves *something,* and that does not have to be a direct sale. Your next step could be a gift or an invitation: offer the person your lead magnet, for instance. That's a great way to build your online family, while also testing whether your lead magnet compels people to opt in. However, make sure that you tell them exactly why you're offering them the lead magnet. Ask before you send the gift or invite, and drop the link only when they say "yes".

Most importantly, keep the conversation going. They'll know you're not a selfish and transactional individual but someone who genuinely displays interest. Who knows, you might even make a sale due to their curiosity and land the most loyal customer of your business. At the very least, you'll have made a new friend!

When Bo and I were talking about her Active Organic Marketing, she said she's now built her muscle memory. Each time she sees a post, when she reaches out, she doesn't agonize over each response any more. At any point, she can feel confident, because the whole point of her reaching out is to help other moms.

"How long do I keep up with this?" is a common question. We understand how making so many conversations with a strategic intention can get draining. I definitely felt that way, especially because my introversion has a limited social battery. You'll have to keep this up until you're confident that you could really nail exactly who your ideal buyer is – to the point where you would literally put money behind it. By using your knowledge to invest into advertising. Then, the personal interactions can dial down a bit, with selective responses. As a beginner, focus on your organic activity.

OUTREACH SYSTEMS AND PROCESSES

Part of the point of active *organic* marketing is that it flows *organically.* You've probably got one of those cheesy canned messages that make you cringe at how robotically corny it sounds. However, you want to establish a systemized approach to identify the common threads that weave into and tie your ideal customers together. Think organic, yet not completely random. These common threads are an invaluable asset to have on hand when you start to build your paid ad campaigns. They help you decide what audiences to build, what wording to use and how to position your offers. With our organic outreach for our skincare business, Bona and I started with the demographics of our ideal customers and a broad need around skincare. Single women in late 20s early 30s, moms in late 20s to mid 30s, moms in late 30s to 40s and women who were partnered with no kids; all of whom wanted affordable natural skincare products.

As we had real conversations with real women in these broad categories, we were able to collect real stories and intel on the problems they were facing, the aspirations they were working towards, other interests they had and what they spent most of their time doing. And we wrote it all down, grouping together the common themes.

How they described their problems and aspirations helped us craft the words for our ads and what products or lead magnets we wanted to feature. Their various interests (e.g. home decor, yoga, Pilates, astrology, pets, plants, travel, literature) and what they spent time doing helped us build different audiences to target.

Getting this deep insight into your ideal buyers is the biggest gift from the hard work of doing organic outreach. Because it will enable you to start scaling all that work quickly, easily and cost-effectively with paid advertising.

Running paid ads as a new business still requires a lot of testing and quite the learning curve, but starting with the foundation you've built from active organic outreach means you can shorten this learning curve.

PHASE 4:
SCALING WITH PAID TRAFFIC

"I'm scared to try ads." "I ran ads but didn't get any results. What did I do wrong?" "My ads were doing so well. And then, they weren't. What happened?"

These are the most common questions and comments I get from clients when it comes to paid advertising. Chances are you're also in one of these buckets. The bad news? There's no silver bullet when it comes to ads. (And don't believe anyone who tells you there is!) The good news? Anyone can run ads successfully with the right mindset and approach.

THE RIGHT MINDSET

The biggest mistake people make when running ads is expecting sales straight away. Whether you're just starting out with new ads or optimizing ad campaigns that are already running, you have to remember that most customers have to see an ad *at least* 5 to 7 times before buying. With our feeds as saturated as they are, it's more like 12 times that someone needs to be exposed to your offer before they purchase. Unless that customer is already solution-aware.

Paid ads, especially early on, are an investment to collect data on what works and doesn't work with your target audience. Yes, eventually, you'll have a well-oiled machine that will get you at least $4 back for every $1 you put in. But it takes time and work to get there. When I started running paid ads for our skincare business, I *still* fell into this mindset trap. Even though I had worked on so many client ads accounts before and I coached my clients on this mindset, I somehow still expected things to be different for me and to start converting on auto-pilot straight away.

I remember feeling frustrated and disappointed about not getting *results*. And then I realized I had a very narrow definition of results. I was fixating on immediate sales from a completely cold audience instead of focusing on what the data was telling me so I could refine my ads to warm the audience and *then* convert them. Once I shifted this focus to a test-learn-tweak approach, I got the results and sales I had wanted.

THE RIGHT APPROACH

So, what do I mean by a test-learn-tweak approach?

Test: It's all about starting with a set of creative elements (images, videos), ad copy, offer and testing each combination with your target audiences.

Learn: Then you look at your metrics and analyze what the data is telling you. Which creative elements are working really well? Are your images and videos not stopping the scroll? Is your ad copy enticing customers to click through to your website? Which of your audiences are taking action?

Tweak: Based on what you've learned, make changes to your ad campaigns.

Businesses that are new to paid ads (especially) require a lot of testing, and the process is *quite* the learning curve. But starting with the foundation you've built from active organic outreach and the insights it gives you on your customer means you can drastically shorten this learning curve.

And even when you have your well-oiled ads machine, you can't set and forget. You need to keep experimenting with your creative elements, how you target your audience, the words you use and the offers you make.

This reminds me of one of my clients who had been running paid ads for years. They had enjoyed a regular return on ad spend of 3.2 (which means they were earning $3.20 for every $1 they were spending) but it was starting to inch down.

I reviewed their ads manager and realized their target audiences were tapped out and they hadn't created new imagery or ad copy let alone tested it.

Because I had already worked with them on their traffic pyramid – helping them makeover their social media for passive organic marketing, collaborate with selected influencers to leverage their audiences and build a small but loyal community of raving fans from active organic marketing – I had a rich base to dip into.

I collated the user-generated content that their customers and influencer partners had shared and used it as my ad creatives. I created new target audiences based on the other interests their community of fans frequently shared about. I wrote ad copy in the same vein as the organic conversations they were having with their customers.

I tested. I learned. I tweaked. I repeated.

And the results spoke for themselves. Their return on ad spend went from 3.2 to 7.8 in 3 months.

TRACKING YOUR SUCCESS

Once you have established your social media platform and start pushing content that attracts traffic while giving you sales, you know that you have meticulously followed each step on the ladder. However, your journey doesn't end there; this is just the beginning. Your traffic generation, sales and scaling up are all intertwined for the rest of the life of your business, because these are the threads of its fate. How do you know you're making progress and improvements organically, by involving influencers, with paid ads, and using other methods? You have to have something that shows you figures to keep stock of. Yes, tracking your success is an essential step that you will be doing regularly to keep a check on your growth rate, expenses to growth ratio and many more metrics.

In the previous section discussing magnetizing your audience, you learnt the various kinds of lead magnets to attract your ideal audience by offering them something of immense value, ranging from giveaways, to the Live Conversion Method™ sessions. You can use codes, affiliate links, or track traffic to a specific landing page setup for that partnership. Take note of which of your lead magnets is driving traffic and which isn't. What audience do your partners or influencers have? What content are they posting? How regularly do they talk about you?

For your paid ads, use the tools on your social media's marketing dashboard or ads manager console to check out metrics that show you:

1) **Purchases or Conversions:** This belongs right at the top of your list. Because everything else is just a vanity metric if your ads and landing pages aren't resulting in the number of sales you're aiming for.

2) **Cost Per Result :** How much is each *result* that you have set your ad up for (whether that is a click. a sign-up or a purchase) costing you? This will help you understand your current cost of a lead or conversion.

3) **Click-Through Rate (CTR):** Of people who see the ads, what % are clicking through to take the next step (whether that is to your landing page or other linked pages)? This will help you understand how effective your ad copy is at compelling your audience to click through.

4) **Engagement:** How is your audience interacting with your ad? Are they clicking on the link, sharing, liking, saving or reacting to the post? This will help you understand how much social proof your ad has.

5) **Reach:** Reach shows you how many people see your ads in a timeline.

6) **Impressions:** Impressions show you how many times your ad was viewed. Multiple views by the same account counts as an impression but not as a reach.

7) **Clicks:** Clicks refers to people clicking on your CTA that you mention.

To know which of these metrics work for you, you'll need to make your own benchmarks, with the help of:

- The industrial average benchmarks
- The economics of your brand
- The historical growth of your business

Once you see the shifts on different ads, lead magnets and organic growth techniques, you'll be able to chart out your "keep doing more of this" and "never doing this again" methods.

KEY TAKEAWAYS

1) The Traffic Pyramid is a way for you to build your own audience of ideal buyers without spending any money on ads.

2) Ideally, you'll move in a step-by-step fashion from *Passive Organic Outreach* to *Paid Ads.*

3) The data and audience you'll collect from the first three tiers enables you to not only earn money, but you can apply your knowledge to your paid strategies to shorten the learning curve and to not use your money to find your audience. In other words, generate traffic and sales organically before moving to paid ads.

4) The first step is to determine which platform/s works best for you, and then explore and master the functionalities within it. Choose the platforms your audience are already on.

5) Master one "meet demand" and one "create demand platform first, and only then do we move to another.

6) To build your audience, think like the owner of the platform as a host, and connect with the influencers, who are like the "life of the party".

7) You can get an audience by posting great content and leveraging other people's audience, like Influencers and List Builders, through collaborations.

8) Start with paid ads once you already have a decent customer base and/or know your audience in detail.

9) Keep track of your success using metrics such as CTR, PPC, engagement, reach and clicks by setting up your own benchmarks.

Actionable Steps:

1. Once you're settled on what platform works best for you: explore all the tools, features, and functions of the platform.
2. Find the right message and story for the audience based on the *symptom-aware, problem-aware and solution-aware* approach.
3. Leverage other people's audiences by reaching out to influencers to promote you, your lead magnet and/or your product.
4. Actively reach out to individuals who you think are an ideal buyer. Not only will you get actual sales, but you will be able to learn so much about them that can start to inform your paid advertising!
5. Scale up by using paid ads when you have a decent-sized customer base, or you've done active organic outreach effectively to know your audience's specific interests and behaviors. Always track your success and go in with the mindset of learning, testing, tweaking and repeating.

BECOME A GROWTH HACKER

So, we're at the end of our time together (for now!) Thank you so much for reading The Traffic Formula!

Now that you've learned how to identify your audience, magnetize them with the right lead magnet and master your Traffic Pyramid, you've got a foolproof strategy to multiply your cold traffic.

But this is not Goodbye! In the next book, I'm going to build upon the Traffic Pyramid and use emails and the Live Conversion Method™ to supercharge conversions en masse.

Also, if you are ready to put what you've just learned into practice, then I'd love for you to join me for my Free 3-Day Cold to Converted Challenge which I host in my private Group on Facebook, E-Commerce Growth Secrets with Deirdre Tshien.

I show up Live with free training on how to implement all these strategies and you get to do it all in a supportive environment with hundreds of growth-obsessed E-Commerce business owners just like you.

Register at TheGrowthBoss.Com/Challenge. See you on the inside!

ABOUT THE AUTHOR

Deirdre is the creator of the Live Conversion Method™ and founder of Growth Boss Academy, a leading mentorship program for e-commerce business owners wanting to scale to multiple- 6 and 7 figures using the power of tribe-building, funnels and human connection.

9 798734 247143